THE ART OF
CELEBRITY
SERVICE

THE ART OF
CELEBRITY
SERVICE

ERIC WILDER

iUniverse, Inc.
New York Lincoln Shanghai

The Art of Celebrity Service

iUniverse books may be ordered through booksellers or by contacting:

iUniverse
2021 Pine Lake Road, Suite 100
Lincoln, NE 68512
www.iuniverse.com
1-800-Authors (1-800-288-4677)

ISBN-13: 978-0-595-40165-9 (pbk)
ISBN-13: 978-0-595-84543-9 (ebk)
ISBN-10: 0-595-40165-1 (pbk)
ISBN-10: 0-595-84543-6 (ebk)

Printed in the United States of America

This book is dedicated to all of the wonderful employees of Almaden Valley Nursery, who, for the last thirty years, have gone out of their way to make our customers happy and who have worked with a sense of pride and purpose to make every day a special day and every shopping experience a memorable one. Thank you for helping to create something we can all truly be proud of.

CONTENTS

FOREWORD

I first discovered Almaden Valley Nursery in June 2004. I had taken a job at a local high-technology company in San Jose, California. It was summer, my favorite time of year. I was far from home and I missed my garden, so I decided to plant some vegetables in pots.

A quick search of the telephone directory yielded a handful of nurseries. Almaden Valley Nursery was nearby, so I called for directions. The woman who answered the phone cheered me with her upbeat greeting and I laughed aloud when she asked, "How can I make your day?" She assured me that they had the particular brand of organic fertilizer I wanted and, within minutes, I was on my way.

The nursery sits by the side of a busy, six-lane expressway in south San Jose. Traffic was backed up on the expressway with people waiting to get in. Ordinarily, I wouldn't wait, would have even skipped the trip to the nursery, but the memory of the cheerful voice on the phone, along with the long line of cars waiting to get in, made me curious. From the moment I entered the nursery, I knew it had been worth the hassle.

The sound of flowing water and a life-size mural of a spectacular waterfall greeted me as I entered. For a moment, I wondered if the mural was real because the sound of the waterfall drowned out the expressway traffic. A quick search revealed a fountain tucked behind some plants. I was enchanted. Who had designed such an intriguing entryway? Did he or she know the effect it had on customers? And, most of all, what was the rest of the nursery like?

As I ventured into the plant area, two employees greeted me on their way to helping other customers beyond the shade structure. One of them pointed out a particularly beautiful flower I didn't recognize and mentioned that it looked stunning next to another plant that I did recognize.

That was my first customer experience at Almaden Valley Nursery and it left me wanting to return. And, return I did, several times that summer, even after I had finished planting and had no room left for more. I went back because Almaden Valley Nursery fit the vision I had had a year earlier of how a highly successful nursery might operate. It was a place of wonderment with its beautiful layout, gorgeous plants, and ever-so-pleasant-and-helpful staff.

The previous summer I had worked in a nursery back home and had thoroughly enjoyed it, in spite of the nagging thought that something critical was missing on the customer service end. I have a background in marketing and customer service, so I approached the owner and offered my expertise. I had a vision of what that nursery could become, given a targeted focus and marketing strategy. Although the owner realized that he needed something to change, the transition required a radical shift in mind-set, something neither he nor his staff could easily make. By summer's end, I'd begun to think that perhaps my vision had been too idealistic.

Then I discovered Almaden Valley Nursery and met Eric Wilder, the owner and driving force behind the nursery's Celebrity Service Experience. It was an epiphany and I was an idealistic (and very happy) Pollyanna again.

If you are like most consumers in the United States today, you've experienced your share of poor customer service. You know what I mean—employees who are disinterested, disconnected, discourteous, slow to respond, or just plain rude. They take up space waiting for a paycheck they believe they have a right to receive simply for clocking in and standing around, and the management's behavior generally is a reflection of theirs.

This shoddy customer service is evident not just in retail, but also in most industries. It's reached epidemic proportions in many companies that provide telephone customer service. So, a company like Almaden Valley Nursery stands out like an oasis in the desert.

If you're like most people, the Celebrity Service Experience is unlike anything you've ever encountered before, and to paraphrase Eric Wilder, "It will make your day."

If you're an owner or manager of a business, you *must* read this book if you want to stay ahead of your competition. If you want a fresh perspective, a way to inspire your managers and your employees, and a way to Make Your Customers' Day, every day, the Celebrity Service Experience is what you've been looking for.

Eric and his management team have worked long and hard to develop this program, and their results are phenomenal. The Celebrity Service Experience sets the standard for customer service across the board by putting the customer at the center of everything that you, as a businessperson, do. It's a program. It's a standard for excellence. It's a new way to do business. Once you've experienced it, you'll refuse to settle for anything less.

So step right in, turn the page, and enjoy. May the Celebrity Service Experience inspire you as it has inspired me.

CJ Morgan
Marketing Consultant
June 2005

ACKNOWLEDGMENTS

I have been fortunate to be part of the retail nursery industry for more than twenty-five years—an industry in which members are open with their peers, share information, and spur one another to continuously improve by challenging each other.

Over the course of my career, many people have touched my life. I would like to thank CJ Morgan for encouraging me to write this book and for the countless hours she spent in the editing and layout. I really appreciate all of your input and advice.

To Kellee Magee who helped me get my first magazine article published, you took it to the next level and helped to stimulate my writing and speaking career.

To Ian Baldwin for helping to guide our company, thank you for motivating and challenging me to raise the bar and reach for new heights.

To Preston Oka for supporting and encouraging me when I was a young buck, you taught me how to talk less, listen more, respect others, and be patient. (I'm still working on the last one.)

To Ron Kanemoto, my good friend, for all the wisdom you've shared with me over the years, your honesty and unique insight about business and life, and for all the good times we've shared. (Hope there are many more.)

To Gary Strutz for all of the personal time you have given me and your invaluable input and guidance in my business and personal life.

Our company would not be what it is without great management and great employees. To Matt Lepow, Steve Mihelitch, and the rest of our team, thank you for your loyalty, enthusiasm, and participation in the journey to make Almaden Valley Nursery one of the best garden centers in the country.

To my mom, Janine, whose unconditional love and support in all of my endeavors has given me the opportunity to do things many only dream about.

To my beautiful wife, Lolli, and daughter, Alena, whose constant love gives my life meaning. I could not do this without your support and encouragement. I have to be the luckiest guy in the world to have both of you in my life.

Finally, to God, who makes all good things happen and without whose grace this book would never have been possible.

Eric Wilder

INTRODUCTION

It's funny; I never set out to write a book—it just sort of happened. Over the course of a business career you tend to go through a process of learning, creating, and then sharing. It's all part of a cycle. Over the last twenty-five years, I've had the opportunity to learn from the best owners, managers, and companies in the retail industry. Along the way I've had mentors who have taken the time to impart their wisdom to me and who have cared enough to help me grow both personally and professionally.

I look at it kind of like this: life is full of teachable moments, and in order to be successful you have to be ready when opportunities come your way. I'm always taking notes or scribbling down ideas. I have this file drawer, and every idea I get goes into it. I file them under categories and if I need to, I create a new category and start another file.

I'm constantly reviewing these ideas and looking for ways to apply them in business. From the very beginning I tended to look at an idea and say to myself, "That's great, but how can I make it better?" Our company is an amalgamation of original ideas that have been created with the help of our employees, and ideas I have picked up in my travels across the country while touring other businesses.

If you were to walk with me through our garden center I could literally point out dozens of ideas I have picked up elsewhere and applied in a unique way to our business. And that's what makes life interesting. You never know where or when you are going to find that next idea. But you have to be willing to act on it, to do something about it. That's what sets successful companies apart in the marketplace.

The San Francisco Bay area is one of the most competitive retail markets in the country, especially in south San Jose. The demographics are all over the place with minorities now making up the majority population. It's a virtual melting pot of different cultures. Everybody wants a discount and every major mass merchant and discount chain can be found within a couple of miles of our business to give it to them.

I knew from the beginning that in order to get the prices we needed to survive and grow in our market, we would have to not only make our place look special, but make the shopping experience special as well. So we applied what I had learned, and over time we became successful. Aristotle once said, "We are what we repeatedly do. Excellence, then, is not an act, but a habit." We keep working on things until we get them right, and then we work on them some more.

Now, we're certainly not anywhere near the biggest garden center in size or volume. In fact, we operate on a fairly difficult one acre site. But we are progressive and unique and we have learned how to make the most of our situation. And word about us has gotten out. We draw customers from all over the Bay Area. Some of our customers will travel more than two hours just to shop with us. Garden center owners from all over the world come to visit us to see what we do. And we share our ideas with them so they can continue to improve and grow as we have.

I really enjoy sharing and teaching what we have done at the nursery. I enjoy seeing others implement our ideas and succeed. Besides, duplication is a great form of flattery! I remember all of the times people have helped me. Years ago a good friend in the nursery industry said to me that he didn't mind if I used some of his ideas as long as I would share my own ideas with others if I was ever in a position to do so. It's all part of that cycle.

Eventually I was asked to write articles for industry trade magazines and newsletters and then I started getting speech requests. After some time, you build up a pretty good collection of ideas. In the back of my mind I always thought, "Someday I'll put this all in a book," but I never really thought about it seriously. And then as luck would have it, someone read one of my articles one day and said, "Hey, you should write a book!"

And I thought, why not? It's an opportunity to give something back the way others have given to me. So here it is. I hope you enjoy it and find it helpful, and that it expands your way of thinking. You will notice that the action steps at the end of each chapter can help you implement what you learn, because the ideas won't help you much unless you put them into action.

And if in fact they should prove beneficial to your business success, I encourage you to share your ideas and success with others as well. Keep the cycle going, pay it forward. And do it all with a cheerful heart and a loving spirit, because at death we will not be judged by the amount of work we did, but by the amount of love we put into it.

How It All Began

More than thirty years ago, my father Erwin Wildermuth left a secure management position at a landscape construction company to follow his dream of owning a garden center. In 1973, he bought a one-and-a-quarter-acre horse ranch and moved our family to the outskirts of south San Jose. Two years later, the horses were gone, the stables had been removed, and the property had been graded and paved. My father had transformed the former horse ranch into a retail garden center.

It was a true mom and pop business. My parents worked seven days a week. We had no employee training program, no customer service policies, no merchandising, no displays, and no profits. As a kid, I watered plants and helped customers load their cars. I even did general maintenance work, but my heart just wasn't in it. My lack of plant knowledge intimidated me when I had to help customers. Besides, I had bigger plans. I wanted to work in the music industry. At sixteen, I went to work at a record store in the local mall where I was exposed to merchandising ideas and advertising. I eventually worked my way up to an assistant manager position and our store quickly became known for its outstanding merchandising displays.

After four years away from the nursery, I came back to the family business to help my parents. A few more years passed and the nursery was still struggling. In 1988 it became apparent that changes were needed. I wanted to give running the nursery a try, so I convinced my dad to allow me one year to run the nursery to see if I could turn things around, and he agreed.

I soon came to realize that to grow the company I would need to learn a lot more about how to operate a garden center. I made every effort to visit our local competitors, attend business seminars, read books and articles on retail, and gain advice from my peers (who were more than willing to share). I also came to realize that the best ideas could be found and transferred from other retailers and businesses, not just the nursery industry. Whether it is a bank, hotel, travel agency, or a car dealership, you can take away a learning exercise from just about anybody or any experience—*you just have to look for them.*

We actually achieved a profit that year, and twelve years later, after continuous remodeling, and hiring and training an exceptional staff and management team, we had become one of the better known and more profitable garden centers in the United States. We host garden center tours from many countries every year. People visit us from all over California just to see the nursery. Yet, in spite of our success, I still felt that something was missing. I was looking for that something special that would help us truly stand out, not just from other garden centers, but from other retailers as well.

Most retailers (especially garden centers), tend to promote one or both of two customer value concepts to consumers: the best price or the greatest selection. But what about service? Businesses that promote service invariably tout their knowledgeable employees. The problem is that you never seem to be able to find those employees when you need them.

The other problem is that no matter how knowledgeable your employees are, if they aren't motivated or trained well, or don't have a customer service-oriented personality, they won't be good at helping your customers (nor will they be fun to work with). The more service horror stories I heard, the more strongly I believed that service was the key. I went on a quest in search of how to implement the best possible customer service. The answer to my quest came to me in a most unusual way.

One day my wife, Lolli, and I were in southern California shopping at a well-known women's clothing store in a trendy mall. We were dressed in fairly casual clothes and most of the sales staff didn't even acknowledge us. Yet when someone well dressed entered the store the staff approached her immediately. They were extremely helpful and friendly, making suggestions, telling the women how good they looked, and generally fawning all over them. The well-dressed customers were treated like royalty and made to feel special, while my wife and I were ignored and treated as if we didn't matter at all. We almost walked out, but we liked the clothing styles at this store, so we decided to persevere.

I thoroughly enjoy picking out clothes with my wife and I had started a collection for her to try on. I asked one of the saleswomen if she had any suggestions for accessorizing the outfits. All of a sudden she took some interest in us. Once Lolli had tried on some of the clothes and liked them, I started a pile to be purchased. Suddenly, the rest of the sales staff began to pay attention to us. They told my wife how pretty she looked and how great the clothes looked on her. They poured on the positive affirmations to no end and it made her feel great. We felt like celebrities.

And then it hit me. What if we could make every one of our customers at Almaden Valley Nursery feel like celebrities, consistently, every day? My wife and I had just experienced both ends of the customer service spectrum. Our goal at the nursery would be to make every one of our customers feel special whether they were buying something or not.

I already had a friendly, well-trained, knowledgeable staff that was motivated to excel. All I had to do was give them a more purposeful direction. So my management team and I set out to create a place where it would be obvious to *all* of our customers that we care and take pride in what we do. A place where our employees work together as a team that is dedicated to giving our customers a wonderful, fun-filled, personalized shopping experience every time they visit us.

A team that goes out of its way to make our customers feel special. A place where all of our customers feel like—a celebrity!

It's such a simple concept, yet it's one that is seldom experienced. Here is how we did it: the planning, the strategy, and the actual implementation. This is not a book that provides examples or observations about other successful companies. This is not a book about a new type of super fantastic gizmo. This is a book about how to create a system and infrastructure that will enable your company to perform above and beyond your competition. This is a book about how to offer service unmatched in your particular industry. Anyone can do it. It doesn't matter if you are an accountant, car mechanic, travel agent, bank, hotel, church, or other business or organization. You just have to care enough to take the time to do it—every day. It's the Celebrity Service Experience.

CHAPTER ONE

FIRST IMPRESSIONS

Ready for Company

I remember as a child having to clean up my room and help my parents spruce things up around the house when they were planning to entertain friends. I would ask my mother, "Why do we have to make the house so clean?" and she would reply, "Because company is coming over." It's the same in business, especially in retail. The only difference is that company comes over every day of the week.

When you open the doors of your business each morning, are you ready for company? It takes a customer an unbelievably short time to get an impression of a place, *especially* a bad one. First impressions are important to most customers because the way you look creates an expectation of things to come. It can raise expectations and excite a person with anticipation of his shopping experience or it can make him think he made a big mistake long before he ever encounters an employee. Your store or business actually begins when your customers first see your store and think about you.

Many people also have certain shopping fears based on previous experiences. When entering a business, some people worry they might not be comfortable in your store. Some people fear they may not understand what you tell them. The cynics of the world worry that they won't believe what you tell them. Others are afraid you won't relate to their needs. Worse yet, there is a natural, built-in apprehension that the products they buy from you might not work or satisfy them. The challenge is to address your customers' expectations, as well as their shopping fears.

Most companies display their store hours at the entrance, but it is amazing how few have a welcome sign. Are the day's incoming deliveries piled up in front of the entrance? Is the parking lot swept? Is the landscape alive? Are the weeds pulled? Are the floors vacuumed? How about music? So many companies don't have any background music to help relax customers. Or, worse, they play music that might be pleasing to their teenage employees, but repulsive to their customers. Music should set the mood and add to the ambiance, *not* entertain. It should be in the background, almost unnoticeable, not blaring loudly, making it difficult for customers and employees to hear each other.

How about scents? A pleasing fragrance can stimulate the senses and add to your customers' comfort level. In our business, we have to deal with chemical smells and fertilizers. We constantly burn candles or spray air freshener inside our store. We also try to position fragrant plants for sale right outside the transition zone from the store into the nursery. Our products are lined up straight on the shelves and our plants are spaced far enough apart so the customers can actually see and reach the individual plants.

Perhaps the most overlooked area in most businesses is the restroom. How many horror stories have you heard about restrooms? My wife and her friends pass much of their judgment of a business based on the cleanliness and appearance of its restrooms. What do your company's restrooms look like?

We chose to make our restroom a humorous adventure complete with "seat up" and "seat down" instructions. We hired a mural painter to create a comic mural on one wall. We even have a customer courtesy phone inside our restroom like they have in expensive hotels. It doesn't actually work, but it has important, funny phone numbers listed on the handset to amuse our customers!

Our bathroom would not be complete without a sign that reads, "Please wash hands or alarm will sound!" We use the bathroom walls to hang framed prints from our gift shop that don't sell. Below the art hangs a hand-painted fish sign that reads "ugly art that won't sell." That always gets a laugh. Hey, we want to entertain our customers every step of the way. And the discounted prints eventually do sell! By the way, it's a given that the restroom is clean and checked several times each day.

Once your customers have entered your store and have become acclimatized to their surroundings, they will take in first impressions of your employees. Are they greeted by your employees as they encounter them? Are they welcomed, acknowledged, and made to feel comfortable? Is your staff even aware of them? Are your cashiers talking to each other with their backs turned away from your customers? Or are they gossiping about other customers or employees? Are they talking to their friends on the company's telephone or on their own cell phones?

Some companies go to the other extreme by having their employees or sales staff rush to the customer and then hover over them every step of the way. That doesn't work, either. Most people need to have some personal space when they shop. They need time to think and absorb things visually. But they do need to know that you are aware of them and ready to help if they need you.

The art of the Celebrity Service Experience is not just in walking the fine line between helping our customers and giving them space. It's about entertaining them at *their own* pace. We want to create a unique experience for them. To do that, we knew that we would need to commit to the experience 100 percent of the time. We also realized that to be successful, we would have to refresh the experience every day. Since people tend get bored easily, we knew that we would always need to search for new ways to improve.

A lot has been said and written about the new experience economy and how to control your customer's shopping experience. While there is a lot of truth to that, we wanted our focus to go beyond the experience—to the result. If we stage the experience the right way, our work actually becomes a form of art or theater and our customers become part of the play. We want to actively engage each of our customers. Our goal is to hit each customer's emotional sweet spot. The Celebrity Service Experience is all about how we make our customers feel inside. They might eventually forget what they bought from us, but they will never forget how we made them feel.

Standards and Goals

The purpose behind creating and developing the Celebrity Service Experience was to add value to the products we sold in such a way that the products would become secondary to the way we make our customers feel when they shop in our nursery. We wanted to be known for something other than just selling great products or providing a great selection. We knew that if we could identify and then create a standard of excellence that our competitors couldn't match, we would be a step ahead of them.

We needed to set a new standard of excellence and capture that standard in one easy-to-read sentence that our staff could easily memorize. It came to me, quite suddenly, and it was simple, too:

> **"Our standard of excellence is to be exceptional in everything we do."**

That summed it up—something that people would be able to see, feel, experience, and tell their friends about. No matter what the situation, we would strive to perform exceptionally. We printed it on the back of our business cards where it would serve a dual purpose: It lets our customers know what we are striving for and what we expect of ourselves, and every time one of our employees hands out one of our business cards, it reminds them of the standard they need to meet.

We knew that saying we wanted to be exceptional was not enough. We needed our employees to fully embrace our new program. So, we decided to involve them in its creation. This was strategic because it allowed our employees to take owner-ship of the program we were developing. We knew that they were much more likely to be passionate about what we wanted to do if they helped create it. So, we scheduled time in our weekly staff meetings to develop our new program.

I spent a lot of time with my management team in deciding how we would present the concept of the Celebrity Service Experience to our employees. We wanted to make sure that we presented it as a well thought-out plan that would intrigue them.

At our next staff meeting, we asked our employees this question: If you could treat a customer like a celebrity and have fun doing it, what would you do and how would you do it? They could dream as much as they wanted and get as silly as they wanted. Our objective was creativity. After an hour of fun, we threw it at them. This was going to be the new way we would run our company and treat our customers. We now had a team that was excited about our plan and fully embraced it.

At our next staff meeting, we asked our employees to help us set some sup-porting goals to help us pursue our vision. Our focus was on how we wanted our customers to feel, not only about their purchases, but about their shopping expe-rience with us. Here are the five goals we set:

Our Goals

1. To provide our customers with a personalized shopping experience.
2. To provide positive reinforcement to every customer purchase.
3. To help our customers feel good about what they buy.
4. To make our customers feel special.
5. To get our customers to help us to promote our company and our extraor-dinary form of service.

The last one would prove to be most important. We realized that we needed to be deliberate about getting our customers to so thoroughly enjoy their shopping experience that they would tell others about us. This was important because we wanted our customers to be our most effective form of advertising. And they are.

As a result, we haven't purchased any advertising in ten years. In fact, we don't even advertise in our local phone book. The majority of our customers learn about us from other customers. How did we achieve this phenomenal response from our customers? Using the Celebrity Service Experience program, we created an atmosphere that prompts our customers to virtually knock themselves out telling others about us.

Moments of Truth

After we created our standard of excellence and supporting goals, we began to identify all of the situations in which we would be in direct contact with our customers and could apply our goals. These situations are those moments of truth that define who you are in the eyes of your customers.

Moments of truth can be simple or complex, but they tend to be contact points where your customer discovers you, pays attention to you, or interacts with you. The simple ones are things like an advertisement in the newspaper, on the radio, or on television. It can be your delivery van passing someone on the road and grabbing her attention, your business card handed from one person to another, your newsletter, or even your business sign. It can be the company uniforms or clothing you wear and the way you wear them. Even the message on your answering machine can deliver a positive or negative impression.

Generally, simple things create an initial impression like a promise, a hope, or an expectation, but they don't necessarily create a feeling or an experience. If done correctly, they may stimulate a thought, a response, or an action. But they don't go beyond that. We concentrated on identifying all of the situations when our customers might possibly come into personal contact with us.

You can do this exercise during a staff meeting. If you have a large staff, set them up in groups of four. If you have a smaller staff, you can use a white board or a flip chart and do this as a brainstorming session. Ask your staff to list the points when your customers make contact with your company.

We identified **Ten Moments of Truth** or "contact" points for our company:

1. When we answer the phone,
2. When a customer walks through the door,
3. When a salesperson meets a customer,
4. When a customer asks a question,
5. When a customer makes a purchase,
6. When a customer returns a product,

7.   When one of our plants or products fails to grow or perform,

8.   When a promised improvement doesn't occur,

9.   When we deliver a purchase,

10. When a customer enters or exits our parking lot.

These moments of truth became the basis for the Celebrity Service Experience. All of our focus and training, all of our signage, every aspect of how we act, speak, and respond, as well as our presentation of merchandise, centers on these contact points with our customers. We also wanted to identify the things that could potentially—or actually do—annoy our customers, either in our garden center or with other companies.

To do this, we held a meeting with our entire staff to discuss and identify the top complaints that we personally had experienced as customers at other retail stores and those that other people mentioned when asked. We felt that if we could identify the worst problem points and complaints, we would be better able to address them.

We identified **Ten Top Customer Complaints**:

1.   Waiting in line,

2.   Broken promises,

3.   Lack of product knowledge,

4.   Employees saying, "It's not my department,"

5.   Being talked down to,

6.   No visible prices,

7.   Rude employees,

8.   Poor product performance,

9.   Shortage of help,

10. A poor return policy.

Armed with this knowledge, we were now ready to address specific situations that could take place at the Moment of Truth contact points. We were now on our way to creating a program that could prevent a problem before it arose or soften and remedy a problem if one occurred. Instead of spending our time putting out fires, we could now focus more of our time and attention on providing our customers with a consistent, high quality shopping experience.

Chapter One Action Steps

1. **Ask yourself these questions:**
    - ❏ What is your company known for other than the products you sell or the basic services you provide?
    - ❏ What positive things can you do to surprise your customers?

2. **Meet with your staff or key management people and create an answer list for each of the following questions:**
    - ❏ If you could treat your customers like celebrities and have fun doing it, with no repercussions, what would you do and how would you do it? Be open-minded and let your staff be as creative as they want. Challenge them with the responsibility to help implement their ideas.
    - ❏ What would it take to make these ideas happen and how much would it cost you? Also, ask yourself if these ideas have a potential negative side.

3. Make a list of company goals that specifically address your customers' shopping experience with you. These goals will help you decide how to encourage customers to feel the way you want them to about your business.

4. Work with your staff to identify and list all of the customer contact points in your company which create a moment of truth.

5. Review the list of customer complaints above or create one for your own company and discuss ways to improve your operations.

CHAPTER TWO

THE ART OF THE SALE

Customer Interaction Points

How we interact with our customers is at the core of the Celebrity Service Experience. Although this chapter deals with what we say to customers and how we treat them, I want to emphasize that it's not just our words that send messages to people, but *how* we say those words.

Customers retain an impression of their interaction with you from the actual words you speak as well as from the tone of your voice. They also retain impressions of your body posture, facial expression, and overall demeanor. In other words, they know when you're faking it!

We realized that the language we wanted to create would have to be honest, sincere, and believable. The only catch was that we didn't always know what to say, so we developed some scripts, complete with responses and actions, to help us respond positively to any situation. We call these scripts our "Elegant Language Scripts."

To make it fun and to get "buy in" from our entire staff, we included them in the language creation process, too. First, we identified all of the situations where we wanted to create and implement specific Elegant Language. Then, we asked our staff to help us create the Elegant Language for each of those situations.

We identified **Ten Customer Interaction Points**:

1. Phone calls,
2. Greetings (in store),
3. Plant/product guidance and selection,

4. Walking with a customer,
5. Passing by customers shopping a display,
6. Price resistance,
7. Closing the sale,
8. Checkout,
9. Problem solving and returns,
10. When things go wrong.

We reviewed these Customer Interaction Points and then asked our employees to respond to each situation in an elegant or humorous way. We stressed that it was important to develop options for each of these situations so that everyone would feel comfortable using the scripts.

We didn't want our employees to become scripted robots. We wanted them to have as much fun as we wanted our customers to have, because having fun is a credo our company lives by. After all, our company slogan is *"The place where plants and people come to have fun!"*

Now some of the language we use may seem obvious or simple to you, yet the majority of companies don't use it or incorporate it into their culture consistently. Much of it contains subtle nuances that create just the right key to make our customers feel special. The greatest reason for creating Elegant Language Scripts for specific situations is so that our entire staff consistently handles each type of situation the same way. True, there are options for each scenario, but they are consistent, so that all of our customers receive the same treatment without contradictions.

Phone Etiquette

A voice on the phone can be pivotal in affecting a customer's decision to visit your store. We have a little sign above every telephone that states:

Smile before you pick up the phone!

Sometimes the place is packed with customers and we feel rushed and pressured. The last thing we want to do is answer the telephone. That little sign helps us make sure we have the right attitude before we pick up the receiver. Since our customers can't see who they are talking to, we feel it's important to share our names. Our telephone greeting goes something like this:

Almaden Valley Nursery, this is (name), how can I make your day?

(If a customer asks to speak with a specific employee and that employee is not available, we never say someone is busy. That sends a message to the customer that he's not important. Instead, we say the employee is unavailable or with another customer.)

(When placing a customer on hold) May I put you on hold?

(To this day we have never been told no! When we pick up a line on hold we always thank the caller for holding.)

One of the enjoyable aspects about the Celebrity Service Experience is that we always use celebrity names when paging management or our employees.

Telephone for Steve. Clint Eastwood, line one. Clint Eastwood on line one for Steve.

(We repeat the page backward just to make sure all of our customers hear the page. We developed a list of celebrities and placed it by each of our telephones to use for our pages. This alphabetical listing of movie stars, musicians, outrageous celebrities, and athletes from our local professional sports teams helps us select names for our pages.)

A page is always good for a couple of turned heads. Some customers ask us if it really was whoever was announced on the page, others just kind of chuckle to themselves.

Greetings

We make it our goal for *every* employee to greet and acknowledge every customer. That means that as a customer is wandering through our garden center, *every* employee they see or who passes them greets them. Tough, to be sure, but without that goal it will never happen. We want every customer to feel like each employee is delighted to see her and happy she is patronizing our little corner of the world. After all, she could have gone shopping anywhere, but she chose to visit us.

We pay a lot of attention to the body language of our customers, which helps us discern if just a greeting is in order or if we should take the next step and ask them if they need assistance. Most customers will start to look around with more urgency when they need help. They tend to look up and around, not down or at the plants or products. Our standard greeting is probably not too different from anyone else's:

Good morning/Good afternoon, how are you doing?
or
How are you doing today?

It is after we actively engage our customers to help them that we really set ourselves apart. Too many businesses ask questions that can be answered with yes or no. When we greet our customers, we say:

And how can we make your day today?
or
What can we help you find today?
or
So what are we looking for today?
or
Are we having fun yet? Well, let's help you have a good time!

Our staff always says "we," not "I," when we offer to help our customers. This puts the emphasis on the team as a whole, and not on any one individual, because more likely than not more than one employee will be involved before we finish helping someone. It also lets our customers know that we are working together as a team to create their shopping experience.

Product Guidance and Selection

Once we know what a customer is looking for or what kind of planting situation he has, we say things that let him know that what we are about to select for him will be anything but ordinary:

"I'm sure we can find some *special* plants for you today." "I'm sure we can help you find the *perfect* plant(s) for that spot/location." "Let me show you some *beautiful* plants for that spot/location." "We have just the *right* product for you." "We have an *awesome* product that will correct that problem."

We want our customers to know that the plants or products they are purchasing are:

Awesome	Exceptional	Hardy	Nice	Stunning
Beautiful	Exotic	Incredible	Perfect	Terrific
Bold	Fragrant	Intense	Right	Tough
Colorful	Gorgeous	Lovely	Rugged	Unique
Dramatic	Great	Majestic	Special	Wonderful

We place an adjective in front of every plant or product description. We simply don't sell anything that is plain or ordinary!

Walking with a Customer

Our garden center is quite small compared to some, but since we are on more than an acre, we tend to do a lot of walking with our customers. This is when we try to make them feel more comfortable with us. It also gives us a chance to find out how they discovered us. To get the conversation going, we say things like:

"Have you shopped with us before?"
(If they have, we welcome them back. If they haven't, we ask, "How come?" Then we say, "Well, you've been missing out!")

We let them know what sets us apart from other garden centers. We give them an idea of where things are, how to read our signage, and how we can help them.

If a customer says, "This is a wonderful nursery!" we say, "And we're fun, too!"

At this point, we usually offer our customers a Rainbow Pop to suck on while they are shopping. It's our way to butter them up for the rest of their shopping experience. These large, two-inch, all-natural suckers contain real bits of fruit. We go through a pallet of Rainbow Pops each year. We discovered them at a gift show in Atlanta years ago and our customers love them. They go over well with the kids, too, whom we want to have well behaved so Mom and Dad will have a good time and spend more money. We ask our customers:

"Would you like a Rainbow Pop? You know what they say, 'It's more fun to shop with a Rainbow Pop!'"
Our customers are surprised, intrigued, and pleased, all at the same time. And what a way to break the ice!

If an employee happens to walk by a customer with a full cart and he isn't already helping someone, he says:

"Would you like me to get you another cart? I'll be happy to bring those up front for you, so you can keep shopping." We want our customers never to worry about anything other than shopping. We also want them to keep adding to their carts, so this one's a no-brainer.

Positive Affirmations

One of the golden opportunities we have to build excitement and get more products onto a shopping cart is through the continuous use of positive affirmations. What makes us unique is that we take the time to interact with our customers in a fun, nonthreatening way. It makes them feel good about their shopping experience and they recognize that we enjoy what we are doing.

We took some time during one of our weekly staff meetings to develop a list of positive affirmations our staff could use any time they pass by a customer they aren't helping. We challenged them to come up with a positive affirmation for every letter of the alphabet. It wasn't as hard as it seems and our staff had a great time doing this. We use these positive affirmations every day:

- ❑ All these plants to choose from!
- ❑ Bet you haven't seen plants like that in a while.
- ❑ Can you believe the size of the blooms on that plant?
- ❑ Don't those flowers smell great?
- ❑ Dazzling combination!
- ❑ Excellent choice!
- ❑ Fabulous combination!
- ❑ Go ahead; sample the fruit off that tree.
- ❑ Gosh, that's beautiful!
- ❑ Have you seen these new plants we just got in?
- ❑ I have those in my yard.
- ❑ I just love those.
- ❑ I put that plant in my garden recently.
- ❑ Isn't the color on those flowers fantastic?
- ❑ Jazz up your garden with this plant.
- ❑ Just imagine how this would look in your garden!
- ❑ Kudos for choosing that plant!
- ❑ Look at these beautiful plants.
- ❑ Mix these plants together for a great look.
- ❑ Nice choice!
- ❑ No one walks out of the nursery without one of these!
- ❑ Now these would look great together!
- ❑ Oh, you have to have one of these!
- ❑ Personally, I love these.

- ❏ Quite the combination!
- ❏ Really good choice!
- ❏ Smell the fragrance on this plant.
- ❏ Songs were written about those flowers.
- ❏ Super choice!
- ❏ Take a whiff of the fragrance on those flowers.
- ❏ That just says wow!
- ❏ That's a bam!
- ❏ That's a favorite plant of mine.
- ❏ That's a staff favorite.
- ❏ This plant just screams buy me!
- ❏ Those are going to be gone by tomorrow!
- ❏ Those colors look great together.
- ❏ Those plants are pure poetry together.
- ❏ Touch it, doesn't it feel good?
- ❏ Unbelievable!
- ❏ Very good choice!
- ❏ We just love those.
- ❏ Wow!
- ❏ You have a good sense of color.
- ❏ You have great taste.
- ❏ Zebras won't eat those!

Price Resistance

Unless your business is in Beverly Hills, you are going to occasionally encounter customers who complain about your prices. We decided that this was a wonderful opportunity for us to interject humor and to display a little self-confidence and personal pride without showing too much modesty. Many times it's just a customer's way of trying to bring your prices down or trying to make you feel bad because she thinks she is paying too much. If a customer mentions a lower price from another store, we say:

"That's a good price."
(We usually don't get any response from that one.)

If a customer thinks a plant price is too high, we say:

"Yes, but look how happy it is!"

If a customer thinks a product price is too high, we say:

"It's special."
or
"They're special."

Most of the time, these responses get a chuckle and our customer smiles. The more comfortable our employees are in each of these situations, the more positive the experience is for both the customers and the staff.

Closing the Sale

In our business we don't really need to push to close a sale. Our customers usually let us know when they are finished shopping. Our employees aren't on commission, so they don't have to close the deal. For us, it's more about positive affirmations. We want to make our customers feel especially good about the great plants and products they've purchased, so we say things like:

"Wow, these plants look really good together!"
or
"We want some pictures when you're finished."
or
"That looks like a garden on a cart!"
or
"Those colors look great together!"

When the customer is ready to pay for his purchases, the employee who is helping him says:

"Is there anything else we can do to serve your needs today? My name is _____. It's been a pleasure serving you. Here is my card and a few extra to hand out to friends. Please don't hesitate to call me if you have any questions."

It's only at the end of a sale that we personalize it. We don't generally share our names at the beginning of the sale unless asked, because we don't want any appearance that a staff member is trying to earn a commission. After the sale is completed, our sales staff usually hands the customer over to our cashiers by saying:

"This is *(cashier's name)*. He/she is going to take care of you from here and ring up your purchase. Thank you for shopping with us. We hope to see you again soon."

Checkout

Many retailers forget that their cashiers or their carryout personnel are usually the last people their customers see before leaving. These people have the ability to leave a lasting impression. They can put an exclamation point on the experience or they can ruin it, preventing your customer from remembering the great shopping experience she just had. We place an extra emphasis on training our cashiers and carryout personnel. This can't be overlooked if you want to give your customers an exceptional and unique shopping experience that they will remember and tell their friends, family, and coworkers about long after their visit.

We never want to hear our cashiers ask: "Did you find everything you were looking for today?" Instead, they ask:

"Were we able to make your day today?"
or
"Did you enjoy your visit?"
or
"Did you have fun today?"

Our cashier asks every customer:

"Would you like any paper or plastic to protect your car?"

At checkout, we also say the following to every customer upon completing the transaction:

"I'd be happy to carry that out for you."
or
"Can I give you a hand?"
or
"Can I get someone to help carry this out to your car?"

Now it's time to say thank you. There's no rocket science here. If you're thankful for your customers' business and appreciate them, tell them. We say:

"Thank you for visiting us. We appreciate your business."
or
"Thank you for shopping with us. We appreciate your business."
or
"Thank you for coming in. We appreciate your business."

The last thing our customers see as they leave our parking lot is a sign (at both gates) that says:

THANK YOU
For shopping with us.
Please come visit us again.
And don't forget to buckle up!
(We care about you)

Chapter Two Action Steps

1. Identify and list the Customer Interaction Points for your company and consider how you might create Elegant Language Scripts for those areas.
2. Work with your staff to create a list of words that might add value to the products you sell or the services you offer.
3. Create a list of positive affirmations your staff can use to make your customers feel good about the products they are buying or considering.
4. Consider creative ways to thank your customers for shopping with you.

CHAPTER THREE

WHEN THINGS GO WRONG

A key thing to remember is that a problem exists when the *customer* thinks it does. We view problems as opportunities to win our customer's loyalty. A customer has to care about your company and trust you enough to want to share his problems with you. Unfortunately, many customers don't complain when something goes wrong or when a purchase fails to live up to their expectations.

Many people don't think it will do any good to complain, so they don't. Or they may feel like most employees aren't trained to handle problems. For some customers, complaining is a very difficult thing to do. It makes them feel awkward, pushy, or uncomfortable. Some just don't want to take the time to complain. For others, it's just easier to switch to a competitor.

Even when a customer has made a decision to share a problem with you, she still has concerns about how the store's employees will handle the complaint. Will the staff be helpful and courteous? Will they relate to his needs? Will they be quick to address her problems? Will your staff live up to your promise? We try to make sure we give our customers the assurance they need and we try to act with empathy. Our goal is to be reliable and quick to respond. Approximately 85 percent of unhappy customers will return if their problem is addressed, even if it is not solved. Our goal is 100 percent.

Returns

Let's face it; returns aren't fun for us or for our customers. Most customers have a preconceived idea that they will have to fight for a replacement, credit, or refund. And many retailers act like they have been personally wounded when a customer returns a product. This is just plain silly. If you track all of your returns in a year, they usually don't add up to much. If they do, then you have a greater problem. Perhaps your customers aren't getting enough information about the products they are purchasing to help them succeed.

We deal with a living, perishable product in the plants we sell. Most of them don't die on their own. They need help from their caretakers who, nine times out of ten, forget to water them, don't water them often enough, water them too much, or plant them in the wrong location. Only about 10 percent of all returns are related to insects, disease, or a bad plant (we do get some duds occasionally). But it doesn't matter. We want our customers to visit us again. Returns are our moment to shine. So we put on a genuinely happy face.

We want to lower the customer's apprehension and diffuse any potential hostility before it has a chance to build up. We empower each of our employees to handle returns personally within our guidelines. Employees do not need to get management involved unless the customer isn't satisfied with the outcome, which is rare. First, we try to make our customers feel better by letting them know it's not their fault. We say things like:

"You know, that happens sometimes."
or
"Don't feel bad, that's happened to me before."

We follow this with:

"You know, we train our plants to behave, but sometimes they have minds of their own!"
or
"You know, we talk to them about doing stuff like this, but sometimes they don't listen!"

After that we immediately let them know how we can take care of their returns.

"I'll be glad to take care of that for you. If you have your receipt, I can give you a replacement, credit, or refund."

"If you don't have your receipt, I'll be happy to give you a 50 percent discount on a replacement."

"We appreciate the chance to correct this problem for you."

We offer a professional opinion only after the return has been handled. To do so before can make the customer think you are positioning yourself to blame them and then fight them on the return. So after we've handled the return, we say:

"Would you like me to get a Certified Nurseryman to help diagnose what happened?"

To help cut down on returns and complaints, we staple a Return Policy sheet to the receipt of every purchase. It's a type of Customer Bill of Rights. It's designed to provide our customers with a list of all of their options if they want to return something. It explains how we handle exchanges credits, and refunds within a thirty-day time period. We also list what we can do if it was a cash sale, if they paid by check, or if it was a credit card transaction. At the bottom of the sheet, we thank them for shopping with us and we encourage them to tell their friends about our store.

Almaden Valley Nursery Return Policy

Your new purchase just won't fit?
Simply changed your mind?

All gifts and non-plant material may be returned
for exchange, credit, or refund within 30 days.

All items must be returned in saleable
condition with original packaging.

All plants (1 gallon or larger) are
guaranteed in health for 1 year
except for frost or acts of nature.

No guarantee on plants planted in
containers or left unplanted more than
7 days from date of purchase.

Plants must be returned within 7 days.
Nonsalable plants may be returned
for exchange or store credit.

All returns must include store receipt.

Here's what we can do:

If you paid with a Credit Card:
We will credit the purchase amount to your original credit card when accompanied by the store receipt.

If you paid with a Check:
We will issue a refund check from our office within 14 days of your return.

If you paid with Cash:
❑ and your purchase was under $100, we will give you cash back on the day of return.
❑ and your purchase was over $100, we will issue a refund check on the day of return.

Thank You for Shopping at Almaden Valley Nursery

If you enjoyed your visit, please tell your friends!

Unhappy Customers

Occasionally we get a customer who just isn't happy. Maybe he's just having a bad day. We still give him the benefit of the doubt. We ask:

"What can we do to make things right for you?"

If the request is reasonable, we do it. It's that simple. If it is not, we apologize that we couldn't make him happy and then we introduce him to our escort service!

While we strive to provide our customers with the ultimate shopping experience, things do go wrong occasionally. There is no substitute for doing things right the first time; however, when we have an opportunity to correct a mistake, that's when we can really shine above our competition. It has always been our goal to spoil our customers so that no one else's service will do. So why should we act differently when something goes wrong?

We believe that the way we respond to a mistake says more about us than when we do things right. We try to not only make things right, but to dazzle our customers while we're doing it! Our goal is to literally seduce them to the point where they forget about the problem or mistake because of the way we respond.

Usually, after we've offered our sincere apologies, we try to offer a refund (warranted or not) for the amount of the product related to the mistake. For example, if our customer's purchase included plants and five bags of potting soil to be delivered and they received everything but the soil, we offer a refund of the total price of the soil and then deliver it at our expense.

We believe that it's better to spend money to give our customers a refund when they aren't satisfied than to forfeit a lost account for the same reason. After all, who wants to be the person on the receiving end of an error? If we happen to break something on a delivery and for some reason we can't replace it, we not only refund the entire purchase price, we also send them a gift certificate for the same amount to try to get them to shop with us again.

If we make an even larger mistake, we do all of the above *and* send flowers with a card and another apology. The way we feel is that a customer can't send back a bad service experience to be repaired. It's not like a defective product; what's done is done. All you can do is help your customer to get over it in the hopes that it won't be remembered forever in a bad way.

We have been amazed at the response we get from our customers. We get e-mails, cards, and letters telling us how pleasantly surprised they were with our response. On one occasion a customer baked cookies for our entire staff. One customer sent us a fruit basket; another brought us an entire tray of fresh strawberries because we had made her day!

Broken Promises

Many times problems are caused by broken promises, simple things like an employee promising to call a customer back and forgetting. It might be a sales person with a customer saying, "I'll be back in a minute" and returning in ten. Sometimes it's because an employee gives the customer an expectation that the plant or product fails to live up to. Things like "It *will* grow three to five feet in two years." "It *will* fruit next year." "This product *will* make this plant turn green again"—but we forget to mention that it will take three applications before that happens.

In cases like that, we automatically refund the original purchase price (without being asked). If it's a product performance problem, we not only refund the customer's money, we give him another bottle, bag, or box of that product free. In the case of forgetting to call back or not returning to a customer in a timely manner, we will apologize and offer a 10 percent discount on that day's purchase (or when they come in again) to make up for our indiscretion.

Opportunities for Improvement

We know that we can only learn from our mistakes if we see them as steps toward improvement. No one person or company is perfect, so when something goes wrong we look at it as an opportunity for improvement. Every time we make a mistake or have a problem, we track it. We want to know what we did wrong, how we made it right for the customer, and what it cost us. If we have the information, we also include the result. What was the customer's reaction? Did the customer shop with us again?

Almaden Valley Nursery
COMPANY MISTAKES TRACKING SHEET

Date: _____Employee filing report:_____

Customer Name: _____

Problem: _____

_____

_____

Remedy: _____ _____

_____Cost: $_____

We let our employees know that we don't care who was involved with the problem; we care about how it was fixed. When a problem occurs, we review the incident internally with our management team so we can prevent it from happening again. Then we share the results with our staff. If it is a procedural problem, we involve our entire staff to brainstorm solutions or to create a policy that will prevent the problem from happening again.

When we send a letter of apology, we have two members of our management team sign it. We make sure that all of the blame rests with us as ownership and management, and that we accept all responsibility for the problem. We also thank our customers for taking the time to let us know about the problem. Sometimes customers just want to vent so we make sure they have an opportunity to contact us directly if they feel so inclined. It may not always be fun, but by encouraging feedback we create a connection we may not have had before.

Customer Apology Letter

Dear Mr. & Mrs. Customer,

I just wanted to take a moment to apologize for the apparent lack of service and attention some of our employees displayed during your recent visit to our garden center. My manager and I accept full responsibility for the training our employees receive, regardless of their age. While we are dismayed by the service you received, we are heartened by the fact that you felt comfortable enough to inform us about this "opportunity for improvement."

Enclosed is a $25 gift certificate to be used toward a future purchase on any item. This is our way of saying thank you for caring enough to take the time to help us improve. Please feel free to contact me at any time if you want to expand upon the problems you experienced while shopping with us. We are taking active steps to ensure that a situation such as the one you experienced won't happen again.

Sincerely,

Eric Wilder—President

Matt Lepow—Vice President/General Manager

The personal touch of a letter like this from management goes a long way toward soothing a customer's feelings after a painful experience with your company. It tells them that you care, that you understand your shortcomings in that particular situation, and that you personally take responsibility for it. It also lets them know that you're going to take steps to prevent the problem from occurring again. After all, if there is a chance the problem will happen again, why would your customer want to return?

Chapter Three Action Steps

1. Consider ways to simplify your return policy and your return process (the fewer hoops your customers have to jump through, the better).
2. Together with your staff, try to create a list of things to say that will provide empathy to a customer's problem in a fun way.
3. Create an internal policy (along with systematic action steps) to deal with unhappy customers and promises that have been broken.
4. Develop a Mistakes Tracking Sheet to monitor your company's shortcomings and identify areas of repeat mistakes.
5. Develop a form letter for company apologies to customers.

CHAPTER FOUR

IT TAKES TEAMWORK

We couldn't accomplish half of what we do without an outstanding team of employees who knock themselves out trying to please our customers. The key to a great team is hiring the right people and creating a work environment where your employees can grow and thrive. We dislike dealing with petty strife, employee conflicts, or personal problems that affect the rest of the staff. We want to spend our time helping customers and supporting our employees with the tools necessary to do their jobs.

To do this, we need a self-disciplined staff. No matter what the age, every person on our team has an integral role and we trust them to support each other. The hard part is weeding out the potential bad employees from the shining stars. We decided to be up front with potential employees, so we created what we affectionately call our Scare Sheet. This is a paper titled "What It Takes to be an Employee at Almaden Valley Nursery." This paper must be read and signed *before* a potential employee is even given a job application.

The Scare Sheet

> ### What It Takes to be an Employee at
> ### ALMADEN VALLEY NURSERY
>
> **Who We Are**
> Almaden Valley Nursery is a "corporate-run" family-owned business, open since 1975. We are a retail garden center whose product is nursery stock, gifts, and all

other garden-related materials. Our growth depends on repeat customers who respond to a combination of our quality products, the outstanding service they receive from our employees, and the overall satisfaction they get from their shopping experiences with us. We wouldn't be in business without our customers, and we are obsessed with being the best garden center in the business. We consider our employees a "team" and you are our most important asset. This is what we expect from you:

Image
Image is very important to us. We wear our company shirts tucked in and baseball caps are worn forward. Stained, torn, or excessively baggy clothing is unacceptable. Proper covered footwear is required based upon the physical requirements of your job. Visible body piercing other than earrings may not be worn during nursery business hours. Men are expected to come to work with faces shaved, unless they are growing a permanent beard or mustache. It is important to exercise good breath hygiene.

Attitude
We expect our employees to show up for work with enthusiasm and to be consistently on time. We are not interested in "clock-watchers." We expect our employees to ask us "Is there anything else that needs to be done?" before ending each shift and clocking out. We are interested in people who care enough about our customers and our company to "go the extra mile." We encourage and reward employees who take the time to offer ideas or suggestions that might make our company run more efficiently, service our customers better, increase our business, or save us time and money. We expect our company policy to be followed and respected. We expect our employees to take responsibility for their actions. Our employees must be self-disciplined so that our company can concentrate its efforts on supporting our employees and taking care of our customers.

Physical Work Environment
You will work both indoors and outdoors in all types of weather conditions including sun, heat, cold, and rain. Your job is physical and requires frequent bending, grabbing, and lifting. You will be on your feet all day, standing or walking, and throughout you will need to be both pleasant and energetic. NOTE: You will be expected to be able to lift at least a 5 gallon shrub/tree and a 2 cu. ft. bag of soil (on your own). We encourage you to maintain good physical and mental preparedness to enable you to perform your work duties in a consistent, high-performance manner.

Social Work Environment
We have a very social, caring, and outgoing staff. It is important that you are able to get along well with people and the rest of our staff to be a cohesive part of our "team." Our company does not tolerate chronic complainers. We expect our employees to get along with each other. We do not tolerate personal complaints about fellow employees unless their actions make you feel uncomfortable or affect your ability to complete your work properly. We expect all employees to carry their weight and perform their responsibilities in an appropriate, professional manner. In return, we're flexible, and we'll support your growth, both personally and professionally.

Customer Service
As an employee of Almaden Valley Nursery, we expect you to offer our customers polite, prompt, energetic, enthusiastic, and courteous service with a smile. Our employees must have the ability to anticipate a customer's needs before being asked. You need to have the ability to be patient when confronted with a challenge and to continually seek out knowledge about all our plants and products. We expect our employees to act with a sense of urgency toward our customers whose time is valuable to them. The help they receive from our staff should be nothing less than immediate and nothing short of excellent. We strive to exceed our customers' expectations for having come to our nursery. Our goal is to reward our customers with a memorable shopping experience.

Summary
If you feel you have the qualities listed above and can work within the parameters of our company policy and work environment, we encourage you to complete our job application. Thank You.

I have read and understand the above.

Applicant Signature: _____   Date: _____

It's amazing the reaction we get after would-be employees read this. The potentially bad employees just quietly slink out of the store. The potentially good employees usually comment that they are glad to see that we take our company seriously and that we don't tolerate slackers. Most teams operate from a position of strength. You know the old saying, "You're only as strong as your weakest link." We don't tolerate any weak links and we don't want our employees or our customers to have to tolerate them, either.

We have a very thorough interview process that helps us determine if a potential employee has the desire and necessary skills to work for us. After we hire them, our new employees go through a detailed training process with different members of our staff. We go over every aspect of their personal responsibilities with them, as well as the concept, attitude, and responsibilities of the Celebrity Service Experience. Then we ask them to sign our Celebrity Service Covenant.

Celebrity Service Covenant

I will greet every customer with a smile and a warm, friendly voice.
I will acknowledge returning customers by welcoming them back.
I will try to make a connection with every customer I encounter.
I will speak to our customers directly, face to face, especially at checkout.
I will find the answers to our customers' questions to the best of my abilities.
I will make sure that our customers have everything they need to complete their projects.

I will provide positive reinforcement to every customer purchase.
I will ask each of our customers if he/she needs carryout help or help loading the car.
I will do what it takes to make our customers happy.
I will be honest with our customers.
I will invite all of our customers to visit us for their future gardening needs.
I will never forget to thank our customers every time they come in.
I will memorize and speak our Elegant Language and have fun doing it.
I will continue to learn about plants and the products that we sell.

I will be enthusiastic about our plants, products, and company.
I will wear my sucker pouch and carry my business cards at all times.
I will answer the phone and page people correctly.

I feel obligated to help our customers succeed.
I will review the Celebrity Service documents at least once a month.
I will remind myself to be exceptional in everything I do.
I will help my fellow employees by setting the right example.

I have read and understand the policies listed above.

Employee Signature: _____ Date: _____

This may seem excessive, but it works for us. It's the easiest way to impress upon our new employees how important and nonnegotiable the Celebrity Service Experience is to us. We learned years ago not to overlook anything and to be as specific as possible about our expectations. Our system empowers employees to keep each other accountable and to support one another. To achieve the quality of service we expect, everyone must take personal responsibility for our company's performance.

We believe that the Celebrity Service Experience is the result of an attitude and a process, which in turn becomes art. The *attitude* starts with hiring the right people and placing them in the right environment. The *process* brings order to the service we provide so that our employees can concentrate on the added touches that bring the Celebrity Service Experience to life. Since many of the most memorable aspects of our service are creative, what we do becomes *art*.

I want to emphasize that in our staff meetings, we use training exercises that emphasize teamwork. They are simple, fun, and make our employees think about, well…teamwork! One of our exercises is called Green Vegetables. Since we are plant people, I give our employees three minutes to list every green vegetable they can think of. When the time is up we find out who has the most vegetables on their list. Then we cull all of the different vegetables from each of their lists. The total is usually double what any individual employee comes up with. We then emphasize how Together Everyone Achieves More. We created an answer key so we can let the staff know how many other green vegetables they missed between them. This is to emphasize that no team is perfect and that there's always room for improvement.

In another exercise, we ask them to think of situations that depend on teamwork. For instance, consider an armed service unit that has to attack a strategic area. Each person in the unit has to work with every other person. Another team might be a hospital emergency room staff that must work together to provide anesthesia, medication, blood pressure monitoring, and surgical tools, as needed to save a life. Another example could be a fire fighting crew that must work together to put out the fire. In team sports, every player has a role, including the ball boy, coaches, refreshment carrier, and medical team. In synchronized sports like crew, every team member must row in unison.

Then we ask them to think about things closer to home. We ask them to share their own experiences in other places or situations where it was obvious that the employees did not work as a team. We talk about the fact that when someone doesn't do his job or when someone makes a mistake, the customer usually suffers. We also emphasize that mistakes do happen and that sometimes we have to make up for someone else's mistakes to make the team and the company look good. It's like recovering a fumble in football for your own team.

It's even better when you can recover a fumble from your competition. When a customer comes in after a bad service experience with one of our competitors, we have an excellent opportunity to shine. The key to success is to be ready when the opportunity presents itself, because it all comes down to teamwork. Whose team is better, yours or theirs?

Employee Responsibilities

Another thing that enables us to stay so organized is that our employees understand their responsibilities. This goes far beyond the Celebrity Service Experience. To "perform" well, everything has to be well organized. I'm talking about the day-to-day tasks that keep the nursery looking good—the little things that make it all come together. Every employee has a specific area of responsibility to maintain. This helps each one take ownership in a piece of our company that he or she would not otherwise have.

We train our employees to understand what we expect of them, as well as why we expect these tasks to be performed to particular standard. The "why" is critical because when our employees understand why we do things a certain way, it gives them a reason to meet their responsibilities. It provides them with the big picture and helps them understand how what they do fits into the operational aspect of our company as a whole. Here are some examples:

- ❑ Why do we take the time to face our plant or product labels forward?
  Because it makes it easier for our customers to find them and read them.
- ❑ Why do we maintain specific quantities of plants in each row according to size?
  So that the plants aren't crowded and our customers can see each individual plant, making it easier for them to select the plants they want.
- ❑ Why do we maintain our plants in perfectly straight rows in our beds?
  Because it looks better than the jumbled mess at our competitor's store.
- ❑ Why do we deadhead our flowers?
  So they will rebloom more quickly.

We emphasize how important it is to us and to the shopping pleasure of our customers to keep the nursery well organized, clean, and properly signed. And our customers notice. One customer commented that our nursery looks so clean that the trees must ask for permission before they can drop their leaves! We got a kick out of that and it made our employees feel great about the hard work they do to keep the nursery looking clean and organized.

It also goes beyond that. We maintain our appearance standards because it's better for the plants, too. We go out of our way to promote that we have happy plants. We tell our customers that our plants are so happy they bloom out of joy! We promote our nursery from our plants' viewpoint. We tell our customers that our plants get so excited about their debut they fight for space to get on the truck that brings them to our nursery. Our plants are never in a bad mood, and they're guaranteed to make you smile! As a result, our plants have taken on a personality all their own.

We wanted to make sure that every team member would take our requirements to heart and adopt our rigorous standards. To make sure we had the awareness we needed at all staff levels, we developed a program that would continually remind our employees about their responsibilities. We call it **C.A.R.E.**

C.A.R.E. Guide
Concerned Action Requiring Empathy

1. Deadhead flowers, prune, and maintain appearance of plants.
2. Clean up leaf debris and litter.
3. Remove dead or poor plants from beds.
4. Straighten plants in beds and end caps.
5. Restock returned or misplaced plants.
6. Maintain proper quantities in rows.
7. Make sure plant labels face forward.
8. Pull weeds as needed.
9. Put plants away instead of leaving them for someone else to stock.
10. Notify management if you see any signs of insect or disease problems on plants.
11. Water on time.
12. Maintain signage.
13. Remove label holders.
14. Restock customer handouts in information boxes.
15. Rinse dusty plants as needed.
16. Sweep up messes when they happen.

---

17. Clean fountains as needed.
18. Return carts left in parking areas.
19. Keep the dumpster area clean.
20. Stack empty pallets neatly and correctly.
21. Remove broken bags of soil from pallets.
22. Reface and restock chemicals and fertilizer products as needed.
23. Return tools to their proper location in the tool room.
24. Restock paper towels and toilet paper and wipe the sink and mirror in the bathroom.
25. **Take Ownership.**

Employee Training

Many businesses fail due to a lack of employee knowledge about the products they sell or a lack of employee understanding and support of the company's goals. Employees often fail to share the same enthusiasm their management or owners have for the company's products, vision, and direction because that same management or ownership fails to share its vision and goals for the company with the employees!

From the day we first hire an employee, we never stop training him or her. We believe that there is no saturation to education and that everyone can learn something new each day. Our employees must have a desire to learn and they must actively participate in the learning process.

We have a forty point new employee training schedule that covers every aspect of our business, from the products we sell, to how we sell them, to why we sell them. We give each new employee a two-page document with all forty subjects listed on the left side of the pages. The right side lists the trainer for each subject and columns farther to the right leave space for the trainer's initials, the employee's initials, and the date they covered that subject.

Most of our full-time staff helps us train our new employees. This format helps us keep an account of when a new hire is trained in a particular subject or area of our nursery, as well as how well they are trained. If we review an area with a new employee two weeks after their hire date and they are missing a lot of information, we can go back to the trainer and find out if they forgot to share something or if the new employee is just plain "not getting it."

From the first day on the job, we regularly review all aspects of the Celebrity Service Experience with our new employees. We consider this even more important than the training schedule. We review their progress and comfort level with the Celebrity Service Experience and our Elegant Language Scripts on a weekly basis until they "get it."

One of the things we emphasize with our staff is selling the entire project, not just the product. We don't do this with the intention of "add-on" or "tie-in" sales, but from the standpoint of making sure that our customers have everything they need for their plants and projects. The example I give is the time I went to our local hardware store to buy paint for our bathroom.

Three weeks after I completed the project our walls started to mildew. I thought that there was something wrong with the paint, so I returned to the hardware store and asked them what might be wrong. They asked if I had added mildew preventative to the paint before I applied it to the walls. No one had told me that I needed to do this. I was more than a little upset because I had invested a lot of time and money in this painting project for nothing, simply because an employee had failed to tell me that I needed to add a $1.95 packet of mildew preventative to the paint. The store did provide the new paint free, along with the packets of mildew preventative, but that didn't make up for the extra time I had to take to repaint the bathroom.

I developed a training exercise for our staff to help us avoid making a similar mistake with our customers. We ask them to list ten different consumer products that a customer must have in order to use another product. In other words, the first product will not work without the other item. We call this exercise "Products for Products." Here are some of the examples they came up with:

Product	Companion Product Needed
Smoke alarm	Batteries
Car wash	Polish
Lamp	Light bulb
Sewing machine	Sewing needles
Vacuum cleaner	Vacuum bags
Coffee maker	Coffee & coffee filters
Bottle of wine	Corkscrew
Photocopy machine	Paper & toner
Camera	Film
Bird feeder	Bird seed

We want our employees to think outside of our industry because it helps open their minds to things that would seem obvious to most of us. We ask them to focus on the different products a customer might need when making different types of plant purchases. An example for us would be suggesting snail bait with the purchase of young bedding plants.

We realized that how we suggest companion products is important. Instead of asking, "Do you need any snail bait for those flowers?" our employees say:

"Make sure you sprinkle some snail bait around those flowers to protect them."

(At least 50 percent of our customers respond by saying, "Oh thanks for reminding me, which one do you recommend?" or "I think I'm running low. Why don't you add a box to my purchase?")

This approach resulted in a significant gain for our customers. Prior to implementing our companion product process, many of our customers who purchased flats of ground cover or flowers woke the next morning to find that slugs or snails had devoured their plants overnight. Now the plants remain healthy and our customers are delighted to shop with us again and again because they trust us to help them care properly for their purchases.

Most retailers want to achieve the extra sales, but they spend very little time, if any, helping their employees learn how to do this. It's much more effective to teach your employees *how* to create tie-in sales.

We review different sales scenarios that will help our customers better ensure their planting success, product performance, or protect the products they just purchased. We give our employees several different product or project lists at different times of the year. This is one of the training exercises we do at our staff meetings.

This exercise helps remind our employees about the products our customers may need, but may not remember to purchase. We have the products they need to help them succeed so we shouldn't be afraid to suggest them when appropriate. When this is done tactfully, our customers are appreciative and recognize that we are looking out for their best interests.

Staff Meetings

We hold one-hour staff training meetings twice a month. Our meetings are mandatory for all sales and support staff, with cashiers required to attend when requested. We keep attendance records for all meetings and we require our employees to sign them at each meeting. We conduct each of our staff meetings with a sense of purpose. We set specific goals and a desired outcome.

A well-run employee meeting can and should accomplish many things. Unfortunately, many managers make the mistake of trying to accomplish too much. Most employee meetings should either be educational, informational, or organizational. Each type of meeting uses a different format to accomplish its goals.

Educational Meetings

An educational meeting is a training meeting. Use educational meetings to teach your employees new sales techniques, ways to improve communication, or team-building exercises. The format for this type of meeting usually makes full employee participation mandatory. I'm not talking about role-playing. Exercises that teach and require employees to share their thoughts, answer questions, or make suggestions work best for this type of meeting.

We make sure these exercises are fun and thought provoking. Each exercise includes an outline that leaves room for our employees to record their answers and observations. We've developed a file of various training exercises that we rotate on an annual basis. Each year we create or add new exercises to keep the process fresh and interesting.

Informational Meetings

We use informational meetings to share information about new plants or products with our employees. This is the easiest and most common type of meeting to hold. It is a given that we will explain the common features and benefits of new products. We also explain why we've added or would like to add a particular plant or product to our stock. Perhaps it's replacing another plant or product. Or it may provide a better margin or lead to multiple sales or higher consumer confidence.

The benefit to our customers is another important factor we address. And most importantly, we always ask our employees for their feedback because if they don't support the new product, it won't sell well.

Organizational Meetings

We use organizational meetings when we need to update the employees on company policy, our corporate structure, company goals, business strategy, employee responsibilities, customer policy, new projects, or financial information. We also use these meetings to pass on "well dones" to employees or teams and to discuss "opportunities for improvement."

We usually post an agenda for our organizational meetings in the employee break room two to three days prior to the meeting. It's important to keep minutes for this type of meeting and we also make sure we get input from *every* employee during our organizational meetings.

We often split our staff meetings between an educational format and an informational format. Our organizational meetings are kept strictly to organizational topics.

We also try to vary the format of our staff meetings to keep them interesting. Sometimes we provide a simple dinner like pizza and soda; other times we look at slide shows of nurseries we have toured. We strive to make sure that, at least every three months, we hold casual, open meetings with our employees just to share ideas, discuss and address concerns, or answer questions.

We believe that there is no saturation to education and that training is the single most important thing we do. It may be repetitious at times, but we find that it gives us a sense of purpose, builds good habits, and reminds us of our shortcomings. It doesn't matter if you are on the right track; you'll get run over if you just sit there. Remember the quote from Aristotle that I mentioned earlier? He wrote, "We are what we repeatedly do. Excellence, then, is not an act, but a habit." I think that says it all.

Chapter Four Action Steps

1. **Scare Sheet:** Together with your management team, create an employee expectation sheet that clearly defines your company's expectations to potential employees. Make sure you define who you are, the image you want to project, the appropriate attitude necessary from your employees, your work environment, and your customer service expectations.

2. Create a **Service Covenant** with your management team that clearly defines the obligations your employees have to your customers. Have every employee in your company sign the sheet. If someone refuses, let him or her go.

3. Create an **Employee Responsibility Sheet** that clearly defines the tasks your employees must perform for the benefit of your customers. This sheet should have an explanation of benefits to your customers for every responsibility you define.

4. Make an effort to create new employee training exercises every time you read a business book or attend a business-related seminar.

5. Consider ways to make your employee meetings more exciting and get your employees more involved in the actual meeting.

CHAPTER FIVE

IT'S ALL ABOUT THE CUSTOMER

Customer Feedback

Many customers will never let you know that they've had a problem with your service or your products. For whatever reason, they just don't want to be bothered. We realized that the only way we could continually improve and refine the Celebrity Service Experience was to encourage our customers to let us know when we made a mistake by giving them ways to respond.

We also realized that the other side of the equation was that our employees would be delighted to know when they had done something well. It's good for employees to hear praise from their customers and managers. It stimulates them to want to perform the way we ask them to in the first place. All of us respond positively to praise and acknowledgment. Sometimes it's the one thing that gets you through the day.

We strive to get as much feedback from our customers as possible, positive or negative, so we place Customer Satisfaction Forms near every cash register. We also staple a pre-stamped, simplified postcard version of these forms to the Plant Care Sheets we leave with each delivery. This allows us to track everything, from our advertising and our customers' shopping experience, to our staff's performance. We can even track the new products our customers request so we can add them to our shelves.

The key to creating a successful customer satisfaction form is to make it brief, easy to read, and simple to fill out. The last thing a customer wants to do when paying for her purchase is fill out a form.

You also need to consider printing costs, including the type and color of paper. We wanted our survey forms to attract attention, so we had them printed on yellow cardstock. Plain paper doesn't hold up very well and curls over in a handout box. To stretch our costs, we decided to use a five-inch by four-inch postcard-sized form. This would allow us to cut four survey cards out of one sheet of cardstock. We decided to print on both the front and back, so we could include all of the questions we wanted to ask our customers without making the card seem daunting to fill out.

Your goal should be for your customers to be able to complete the Customer Satisfaction Form in less than a minute. Simple yes or no answers work best. If a customer wants to expand on an answer, our form provides room for them to do so, but the idea is that most answers should not require an explanation. Most of our customers' explanations tend to be one-line comments.

We try to cover the level of service customers experience at a number of different contact points with our employees. We also want to know if there is a new or different service or product they would like us to offer. We wanted the last question on our form to be an open-ended one about our customers' shopping experiences to give them an opportunity to provide their ideas and suggestions. And last, but not least, we included space for additional comments. You never know when someone might come up with that one single idea that could transform your company!

Our goal is to deliver such exceptional service that our customers will knock themselves out to give us feedback about their shopping experiences. We want them to let us know what they think about us, about our employees, and about our store and our products.

I'll be honest, we don't get customer feedback every day, but the handful of responses we get each week add up by the end of the year.

Our Customer Satisfaction Form sends the message to our customers and our employees that we want to be held accountable, that we are confident enough with our service to ask our customers for their feedback, and that we are humble enough to accept the feedback we receive.

Customer Satisfaction Form

How are we doing? So that we may serve you better, please take a moment to answer the questions below.

(Circle or fill in the appropriate answer.)
1.   Is this your first visit to our garden center?   YES NO

2.   What made you decide to shop in our garden center today? [ ] Web site [ ] Newsletter [ ] Passed it on the road [ ] Friend, neighbor, relative

3. Did you enjoy your overall shopping experience? YES NO

4. Were you checked out in a timely and efficient manner? YES NO
   If no, how long did you have to wait? _____

5. Was our cashier courteous and friendly? YES NO

6. Was our sales staff courteous, helpful & knowledgeable? YES NO

7. Were you able to find everything you came in for? YES NO
   If no, why not? _____
   _____

8. Is there any other service you would like us to provide?
   _____
   _____

9. Are there any other plants or products you would like us to carry?
   _____
   _____

10. Did you know that we take special orders? YES NO

11. How can we make your shopping experience more pleasurable?
    _____
    _____

Additional comments:

Your opinions are important to us.

Thank You!

Process Checks and Opportunities for Improvement

Although we address any service problems or product issues at the time they occur and at our bimonthly staff meetings, we do a deeper process check each quarter. We summarize the issues by topic and then share them with our employees for their input. The topics usually come from a combination of both our customer survey forms and a list we create of events or problems that occur more than once in a three-month time period.

We devote an entire staff meeting to this process check and cover every operational aspect of our company. This can range from internal things, such as how we process our special orders, how we perform our deliveries, the way we unload and accept plant material, and department responsibilities, to simple housekeeping or service issues like how we perform at checkout, the way we treat our customers, our will-call service, or company policy issues.

Obviously, we hope these issues never come up, but since no one is perfect, we try to limit their occurrence and improve our service if they do happen. If it becomes obvious that certain problems only seem to occur with a particular employee, we speak with that employee in private.

I usually review the issues we plan to address with my management team a few days before the meeting to decide how we will respond. When we meet with our staff, we give them the opportunity to give us input and feedback first. Even if their solutions are the same as ours, we give them credit for them so they have the opportunity to feel responsible for the desired improvement. We only share our solutions if we don't feel comfortable with their proposals. Then we ask for their feedback to our solutions. Although it's extremely rare, there are times when we feel it's in the best interest of our company and our customers to impose a specific response, guideline, or policy. After we've created new guidelines or policies, we date them and ask our employees to date and sign them to show they agree and understand them.

Twice a year we hold a meeting where we specifically discuss our experiences at our competitors or other retailers, restaurants, banks, hotels, or companies that provide a specific service. We ask our staff to come to the meeting ready to talk about two companies that have recently knocked their socks off, and two companies where they have received deplorable service.

We ask them to share the details of where or how the companies excelled and where they failed miserably. We then move into a discussion or analysis of current activities in our own company which might give customers the impression that our staff doesn't perform in the best interest of our customers. Then we ask the staff to think of ideas, messages, or programs that would make customers think we do care about and perform in their best interest.

This exercise was developed by a friend and business associate, Ian Baldwin, a nursery consultant who has advised us for the past twelve years. We have used it ever since he introduced it to us and we always find it very helpful in reminding us of some of our goals.

Defining Customer Satisfaction

We have a unique perspective regarding customer service. Most companies measure customer satisfaction strictly by how satisfied their customers are with what they offer. With this approach, there is no way to track how much your customers actually give up in their shopping experience because they usually will not tell you. If you ask your customers if they are satisfied and do not ask what you can do to improve, you only get half the equation.

We believe that true customer *satisfaction* is the difference between what a customer expects and the type of service or product they actually receive. The difference between what a customer wants and actually settles for is called customer *sacrifice*. The problem with simply tracking customer satisfaction is that it only shows you how well your customers are accepting your limitations. It doesn't tell what they think about the services or products you are *not* offering. We want to be graded not only on what we offer, but also on what we don't offer.

Obviously, we can't be all things to all people. But it helps to keep track of our customers' preferences. This way we can create new strategies for the products and services we *do* offer. Our customers and our competition provide the road map to our success. By listening to our customers and by keeping track of what our competition offers, we can stand out from our competitors.

Doing what everyone else does is boring. Doing what everyone else does and doing it better is a step up. Doing what others don't or can't do is special, and that's what sets us apart. We continually try to break the rules and set new levels for what we do because each encounter between our company and our customers holds the power to enhance or diminish our standing in the marketplace. Each encounter is a chance to stand out and be memorable.

Chapter Five Action Steps

1. Create an easy-to-read, easy-to-fill-out Customer Survey Form. Monitor the results and share them with your employees.
2. Hold specific team meetings to update staff on internal company processes and to address opportunities for improvement.
3. Hold at least two team meetings per year to encourage employees to discuss their personal experiences when visiting competitors and other companies. Make sure you discuss the wows and the shortcomings.
4. Create and monitor a list of all products and/or services that your customers ask for, but that you don't currently offer or provide.

CHAPTER SIX

MANAGING THE CELEBRITY SERVICE EXPERIENCE

For our management team to do its job properly, we need to have a self-disciplined staff that allows us to concentrate most of our time on equipping, supporting, and encouraging our employees. I heard someone once say, "A desk is a dangerous place from which to watch the world." The same goes for management. You cannot manage the Celebrity Service Experience from behind a desk in your office. We manage by using a philosophy called MBWA—Management By Walking Around. It's a management practice that many large corporations have used successfully for decades.

Something special happens when your employees see you in the trenches with them. It builds their confidence in you and they generally rally around their leader. In our company, it also provides a way for our management team to practice what we preach. By working alongside our employees, they can see that we believe in what we ask them to do because we're doing the same thing right along with them. Consequently, they know that we would never ask them to do anything we wouldn't be willing to do ourselves.

When you work alongside your employees, meeting customers as they do, it's much easier to gauge customer reactions to your store, your employees, and your products. You also have the added benefit of being able to observe your employees. Our atmosphere is such that our employees are not bothered by management walking around. They're used to seeing us out there with them and they view it more in comfort than in fear.

Too many managers instill fear in their employees, so the standard reaction when the boss shows up is, "We had better hop to it and get busy. The boss is watching us." This happens for two reasons. Management either fails to hire self-motivated employees so when the boss is not around, the employees goof off, or employees automatically think something is wrong and the boss is checking up on them.

The best way to address deficiencies in customer service is to see what is happening. There's no substitute for being out there. You have to feel the pulse and the pace of what your employees are experiencing. Your employees will respect you for joining them on the front line and your customers will, too.

Instead of hiring official greeters, I think owners or managers should greet their customers. It's like the head of the household welcoming you into his home. You wouldn't send your children to greet your guests; you do that yourself to show your guests how special they are to you. We want our customers to feel comfortable when they shop with us, so we regularly wander through the nursery making sure everyone is enjoying their visit and that they're receiving the help and attention they need.

As a result, at our staff meetings we can better relate to what our staff tells us because we are working alongside them and experiencing their joys and their pain. We've shared their frustration when things get hectic. We can surprise them by showering them with accolades and "well dones" in front of their fellow employees when we've witnessed them doing something outstanding or when they make one of our customers exceptionally happy. Fortunately for us and for our employees, we have reason to praise them a lot.

Managing the Shopping Experience

The whole idea behind the Celebrity Service Experience is to serve our customers in a way that is pleasantly unexpected. Our goal is to do more than our customers ask. We want to exceed their expectations. We want to add value for our customers at every possible opportunity. We try to do this in every area in which we have contact with them.

Samples and Gifts

Everyone loves to receive free stuff. We make sure all of our customers are offered an official Almaden Valley Nursery magnet and a Rainbow Pop. Our cashiers ask them if they received a Rainbow Pop and, if for some reason a customer was not offered one on the sales floor, the cashier gives him one. The magnets are a great advertisement for us, even better than the yellow pages. We figure if our attractive magnet is on the refrigerator, it serves as a daily reminder of the best nursery in town. Our customers never have to look for us in the telephone book and see our competitors' ads again.

With any purchase of twenty-five dollars or more, we give our customers a free gift bag that contains samples of products we sell. The samples for our female customers include potpourri, hand creams, fragrances, and votive candles. For our male customers we provide garden products ranging from plant food supplements, snail baits, hand soaps and men's hand lotions, to inexpensive garden tools. Our cashiers decide what to offer based on the size of the purchase.

We negotiate a lower price for these items in exchange for purchasing larger quantities. Often our vendors donate these samples as a thank-you for the increased sales the samples generate for them. We build the cost of our sample program into the cost of our marketing budget. A purchase of $500 or more earns shoppers their very own "world famous" Almaden Valley Nursery baseball caps.

Dog Biscuits

Our garden center is next door to a veterinary clinic, so many of our customers come in with their dogs. We openly encourage them to do so, but we have signs that say, "Please keep your dog on a leash." The dogs visit regularly and they know that if they behave, they will earn a treat. It's a special touch that shows we care. We keep a box of dog biscuits at the front counter and our regular four-footed visitors know where to take their humans for that special treat. (We always ask the pet owner first.)

Special Orders

Many retailers offer a special-order service, but they charge extra for it. We can't understand why anyone would want to punish a customer when the business does not stock an item the customer wants.

Sometimes it's a matter of timing and we are temporarily out of stock, but our garden center operates on less than an acre, so we are limited in space. We recognize that we can't stock everything our customers want. We try to make it easy for our customers to get the plants or products they want. We scan our vendor availability sheets and provide our customers with the plant size and price prior to ordering. Sometimes we can even offer same-week delivery.

Carry-out Service

Short of a single, lightweight item that can fit in a bag, we ask *every* customer if we can give them some help to his or her car. We have plastic trunk liners and fold-out trays to protect the vehicles from dirt or stains. We are in a messy business but many customers come in unprepared to carry plants and heavy bags of soil in their freshly washed vehicles. We are also short on parking spaces, so you might say we have an ulterior motive; we want to make parking spaces available as fast as we can, especially on busy weekends. Carry-out service is also the perfect way to leave a lasting impression, giving one more employee the opportunity to thank our customers for shopping with us and to encourage them to visit us again.

Deliveries

We even try to make our deliveries exceptional experiences. Unlike many other retailers who make you book a delivery around their schedules, we book ours around our customers' schedules. We have detailed forms for our cashiers to fill out when scheduling deliveries. We ask if the customer would like a courtesy call before we leave the nursery. We make sure the plants are watered prior to delivery, in case our customer isn't at home to receive them. This way the plants aren't half-wilted by the time the new owner returns home. Our drivers leave a stamped, addressed Customer Survey Form stapled to the Plant Care Guide with the customer, or in the mailbox if no one is home.

Thank-you Letters

The final touch of the Celebrity Service Experience takes place one month after the sale. We send all of our large-purchase customers a personal thank-you letter on company letterhead. We log all large purchases over $250, including the customer's name, address, date, the name of the salesperson, and key items purchased. Since the majority of our large purchases are delivered, we don't have to ask the customer for an address. We can also pull address information if they paid by check, although a majority of our customers pay using a credit card. It's not a perfect system, but we don't ask customers for personal information if it's not readily available.

A staff member monitors the logged purchases on a weekly basis to see which customers are due thank-you letters. The letter is a form letter, but it is customizable based on the key items the customer purchased and on who served them. We wait at least thirty days after the purchase date because we want to accomplish a number of things:

1. We hope that by then our customer is enjoying the plants or product they purchased.

2. We want to create a contact point thirty days later to give our customers a reason to think about us again.

3. We want them to know we have not forgotten them and that we appreciate their business.

4. We want to encourage them to feel comfortable enough to contact us if they are having any problems with the purchase.

5. We want to give them a few more business cards and remind them how much we appreciate it when they share their experiences with their friends, family, and coworkers.

Management prepares the letters for the individual employees to sign. This gives us an opportunity to thank our employees again for their sales and service and allows them to personalize letters with their signatures. If a number of staff members were involved in one sale, or if the customer chose to help herself, one of our management team members signs the letter and encloses a few of his or her business cards.

Our objective is to make our customers feel extra special. I know of a few car dealerships that send thank-you letters and even a few doctors and dentists who do so, but very few retailers. It's sad, because customers should never be taken for granted. Our businesses could never survive without them. Here's a sample of our customer thank-you letter:

Thank-you Letter

Dear Mr./Mrs. Customer,

On behalf of Almaden Valley Nursery, I just wanted to take a moment to thank you for shopping with us. We recognize that you have many places to choose from when buying plants and products for your home and garden, so we don't take your business for granted. I hope you are enjoying your Swamp Myrtle and Japanese Maple Trees. Thank you for your continued business.

If you have any questions about your purchases or if there is anything I can do for you at a future date, please don't hesitate to call me. Enclosed are a few of my business cards. Please feel free to share them with friends. Again, thank you for allowing us the opportunity to fill your home and garden needs. It was our pleasure to serve you.

Sincerely,

Matt Lepow—Vice President/General Manager

The Celebrity Web Club

Our Web Club is another way in which we make our customers feel special. It's free and it's available to all of our customers. It's a full-color, electronic newsletter, complete with photos, and it allows us to visit our customers via e-mail once a week. We want to be woven into the fabric of our customers' lives. We want them to interact with us, and the Web Club has become one of the most well-received marketing tools we have ever used.

The Web Club was the brainchild of a very smart, fun-loving, thoughtful guy named Phil Adikes. Prior to creating this weekly electronic newsletter, we sent occasional e-mail messages to our customers to alert them about new plant arrivals, sales, or seminars. Phil sold me on the fact that text messages are, well, boring.

Once we got together and started exchanging ideas about how to make our weekly e-mail communication more interesting, it became a moment of spontaneous combustion. The ideas flowed like water. Our Web Club newsletter not only cross-promotes our Web site, it includes a quotation for the week, sales information, gardening trivia questions, and a lot of photos! We give great prizes to the weekly garden trivia contest winners. We even have an area where customers can provide us with their feedback.

We send the Web Club newsletter via e-mail every Thursday. The club also includes a three-day weather forecast, links to our Web site galleries, a sign-up-a-friend section, garden tips, and a recipe of the week. To further personalize it, we added a Guest Gardeners section. We figure that gardeners love to learn from other gardeners "over the fence," so to speak, so we let our customers know we would like to include articles from them, or even photo tours of their gardens. This allows customers to share what they are doing and gives them a moment of "glory" with our other customers.

We also wanted to give customers a chance to get to know our employees. So each week we include a photo of one of our employees, complete with a personal and very humorous bio and information about their favorite TV shows, movies, music, food, travel destinations, and personal dislikes. This gives our employees a little notoriety, and shows our appreciation for their outstanding efforts. And, it helps our customers recognize employees in the nursery. Our Web Club newsletter fosters a continuing relationship between us and our customers throughout the year.

Having Fun!

Ralph Smedly, the founder of Toastmasters, once said, "The most effective learning is accomplished during periods of fun and enjoyment." We realized from the very beginning that if we couldn't have fun with what we were doing, we didn't want to do it. The key component to everything we do is to have fun. That may sound silly or even irresponsible to some people, but that has always been a driving force for us.

Consumers tend to get bored easily, so they always respond to new forms of shopping and service stimulation. They tend to be attracted to companies in which the employees clearly enjoy themselves while they are serving their customers. We strive to create an atmosphere of fun at Almaden Valley Nursery. It's a place that looks and feels happy, a place where people walk in, feel the excitement, and say, "I want a little bit of whatever they've got!"

A great aspect about having fun is that it helps to diffuse the attitude of those occasional not-so-happy customers—the ones that make the entire staff want to run and hide. These people include the one who may be having a bad day as well as those who are chronically unhappy with everything they do and everyone they meet. The best way to deal with them is through humor.

Humor can be infectious and when we can help turn around a not-so-happy customer, it can only bode well for the next person they meet! I challenge you to attempt to find or inject humor into everything you and your staff do. We have a two-way goal to have "two smiles in every aisle." That means we not only want to present our happy faces in every aisle we walk, we want our customers to be happy, too.

From our Rainbow Pops to our baseball caps to the Elegant Language Scripts, we actively look for humorous ways to surprise and interact with our customers.

Closing Announcements

Even our closing announcements are humorous. You can have a great day with great customers, but there comes a point when the body and mind start to shut down and it's time to go home. Every once in a while, though, we get a few customers who slip through the gate just before closing time.

Sometimes these customers think that because they arrived prior to closing they have the inalienable right to stay for as long as they please. We have a humorous response to these late arrivals. We created some closing announcements that, while very pleasant, definitely give our customers the nudge they need to either buy something or leave. And most of the time, we get a laugh from them.

Attention Shoppers:

The captain has turned on the closing countdown sign indicating our fifteen-minute approach to closing. The captain is expecting an on-time closure at 5:00 PM.

At this time, we ask that you finish any beverages and purchases and bring your carts up front for checkout, so that we can return them to their full upright positions.

Our staff of attendants will be going through the nursery one more time to help pick up items and attend to any last-minute needs.

On behalf of our entire staff, we'd like to thank you for flying our world famous nursery today. We look forward to seeing you again.

Or

Attention Shoppers:

The nursery is open for shopping 359 days of the year, which translates into 2,976 hours of pure shopping pleasure, which should be *plenty* of time to get your shopping done. So please be considerate of our hard-working employees and allow them to go home so they have enough time to get *their* shopping done. We thank you for shopping with us and look forward to seeing you once again.

Or

Attention Shoppers:

It's been another *great* day at Almaden Valley Nursery. Our boss says that next to serving our customers, there's no greater feeling than when it's time to go home to our families. We would like to thank you for shopping with us and look forward to seeing you *and* our families once again.

Throughout the final ten minutes before closing we play a medley of songs with titles like, "It's Closing Time, We're Going Home," and ending with the *Sound of Music's* "Good-bye, Auf Wiedersehen." If that doesn't get them to leave, we play, "Who Let the Dogs Out?"

What can you do to make things more fun in your business? I know some of you will say if work was supposed to be fun, it wouldn't be called work. Sorry, try again. Everyone can use a little humor in his or her life. Your employees will thank you for it and so will your customers.

That's the Celebrity Service Experience in a nutshell. Many of the ideas I have shared here are not new; they are a simple combination of elements packaged in a way no one has done before. Everything we do is a result of our personal experiences. The more experiences we combine, the more imaginative we can be, and the more fun we'll have. I learned long ago that you become what you are committed to, and you have to be passionate about the things you do.

As you have probably figured out by now, this book is not about marketing so much as it is about execution. The marketing comes naturally if we fulfill our promises and execute our service properly. Our goal is not just to satisfy the customers. That goal is far too modest for us. Our company exists to fill a need. Therefore, our goal is to create an environment that will give our customers that special, even crucial, feeling of importance because everyone deserves to be on the receiving end of a memorable experience—to know that they're welcomed and appreciated.

Chapter Six Action Steps

1. Together with your employees, develop (brainstorm) a list of ideas for free gifts or samples you can give to your customers. These gifts might be gender specific and the samples should have the added value of introducing and promoting products you currently sell.

2. Create free, detailed Care Guides for the products you offer. If you offer services, consider creating a brochure loaded with tips about how your customers can get the most benefit from the services you offer.

3. Create a Customer Thank-you form letter that can be sent to either your high-volume or frequent customers. Assign responsibility for monitoring this program to one of your employees.

4. Together with your employees, consider ways to make your Web site, newsletters, working environment, and customers' shopping experience more fun. Discuss these ideas with your employees at least quarterly and create ways to refresh your customers' experiences.

CONCLUSION
LASTING IMPRESSIONS

We have a great employee, Jim Citta, who has captured the essence of the Celebrity Service Experience. Jim is always patient and thoughtful with our customers. He attempts to be humorous in a way that is unique to him. He creates such wonderful experiences for our customers that they send us thank-you notes. In fact, we have lots of great employees who work together and go out of their way to make the customer's day. And we get letters for them, too.

One of our employees, Irene Moreno, gets a great many compliments just for the way she answers the phone. She makes customers feel welcome before they ever set foot in the nursery. One day a customer was stranded at the nursery with her young daughter because her car broke down. Emily Rettner, one of our part-time seasonal cashiers, took the extra time to entertain the little girl until the tow truck arrived. Emily even drew a picture of a unicorn for the child. We received a beautiful thank-you card from the very appreciative mother.

Our Bedding Plant Manager Ferne Watt has to be one of the sweetest people on earth. She is always going out of her way to make our customers feel good and she is consistently mentioned in our Customer Satisfaction Forms. Both our General Manager Matt Lepow and Assistant Manager Steve Mihelitch take the extra time to locate difficult-to-find plants and products for our more "selective" customers and are constantly making sure all of customers' needs are being met. And that's just on the service side of things.

Many of our customers describe our nursery as a "seductive" place. They love the ambience they feel the moment they park their cars. We try to "greet" them with beautiful plantings at the front of the building and with colorful mounds of stuff in pots to pull them closer to examine, touch, smell, and read. We want them to forget about what they actually came in for and become "seduced" by the surroundings.

If we do our job well, customers will forgo an immediate purchase to first wander around to see what new marvels they might pop into their gardens even if they don't have any space remaining for more plants. Our goal is to create a shopping nirvana disguised as a nursery!

We want them to discover our new arrivals and then wander along our concrete paths past the carnival of attractions that beckon to be purchased. Once they're out in the middle of the nursery, we've got them. We make sure our plants are so healthy and colorful that our customers would have to wear blinders to resist the temptation to take them home.

One of our customers describes our plants as carnivorous, sucking every dime from her pocket. Our sales staff members have been playfully described as "plant pimps" and "trained wizards," not only for their knowledge about plants, dirt, garden exposures and growing seasons, but for the wonderful way they make our customers feel. And every one on our staff possesses the ability to carry on an intelligent conversation which makes our customers feel at home and only too willing to part with their money.

We strive to have a visit to our nursery feel more like an excursion or a pleasant field trip than a chore. We want our customers to forget about their plans and what they originally came in for, so they can wander around, drunk with pleasure from the beauty and variety of the plants and products we have to sell.

We want to lead them from the Pottery Plaza to the Shady Hollow, from our Vines that Twine to our Orchard Oasis of fruit trees. Once past the Cathedral of Shade we tempt them with plants in the Collector's Corner. And once they see our tropicals in the Garden Pavilion, they will be further tempted by the Color Courtyard of perennials. You just can't walk down our Isle (aisle) of Roses without stopping to buy color in the Annual Alley next door.

All the while our staff is there, caringly and playfully affirming our customers' selections, loading their carts and helping them along to the checkout counter where they willingly pay the toll for leaving our special place. Our staff knows when to offer help or a kind word and when to leave the customer alone to discover and experience. It's an art that's backed up by a well thought-out process and implemented in way that makes us unique and special to our customers. It's the Art of Celebrity Service. And that's why they prefer shopping at Almaden Valley Nursery rather than anywhere else.

You see, our business is more than selling plants and garden products. Our business *has* to be personal. In this fast-paced world of ours, people need to find that special place they can escape to. Our business is about making people feel good. Our business is about people. Yours should be, too. If everyone just cared a little more, what a better world this would be.

ABOUT THE AUTHOR

Eric Wilder is the former owner of Almaden Valley Nursery, a popular destination garden center in San Jose, California, that was recently selected as one of the One Hundred Revolutionary Garden Centers in the United States. After taking over the struggling family business in 1988, he built it into the progressive multi-million dollar garden center it is today. The nursery is a tour stop for many domestic and international garden center tours.

Eric has more than twenty-five years of experience in the retail industry, and in 1999 he was awarded the "Young Nurseryman of the Year" Award by the California Association of Nurseries and Garden Centers. He is a California Certified Nurseryman and holds an Advanced Certificate. He has served as a board member at the local chapter level for his state nursery association, at the national level for the Retail Division of the American Nursery and Landscape Association, and as a member of the largest retail nursery co-op in the United States.

His unique understanding of today's consumer has given him the opportunity to be actively involved in package design and product marketing for a number of companies related to the green industry. He has also helped put together marketing campaigns for a national wholesale plant grower and a product promotion for an organic plant food company.

Eric has been a guest columnist for *Nursery Retailer Magazine* and has written many articles for industry association newsletters. An accomplished speaker, his passion and enthusiasm for providing better service can be seen and heard in his *Radical Retail* seminars and presentations, where he motivates companies and employees on the aspects of customer service, organizational growth, team building, and big picture thinking.

In his spare time Eric is involved in Christian missions work in his local community and in many developing countries around the globe. An avid outdoorsman, he enjoys hiking, skiing, kayaking, and nature photography. He resides with his family in Idaho.

BOOKING INFORMATION

Eric Wilder is available for keynotes, team coaching, and presentations. If you are interested in a speaking engagement or consultation please visit www.radicalretail.com for more information and contact numbers.

978-0-595-40165-9
0-595-40165-1

Printed in the United States
67121LVS00005B/472-504